In the of Longing

Bilingual Press/Editorial Bilingüe

In the Republic of Longing

poems by
VIRGIL SUÁREZ

Bilingual Press/Editorial Bilingüe
Tempe, Arizona

ISBN 0-927534-89-4

Library of Congress Cataloging-in-Publication Data

Suárez, Virgil, 1962
    In the republic of longing / Virgil Suárez.
        p.   cm.
    ISBN 0-927534-89-4 (alk. paper)
        1. Cuban Americans—Poetry.   2. Immigrants—United
States—Poetry.   3. Exiles—Cuba—Poetry.   I. Title.

    PS3569.U18 I5 1999
    811'.54 21—dc21   99–043656

PRINTED IN THE UNITED STATES OF AMERICA

Cover/interior design by John Wincek, Aerocraft Charter Art Service
Back cover photo by Ed Love © 1998

Acknowledgments

Partial funding provided by the Arizona Commission on the Arts through appropriations from the Arizona State Legislature and grants from the National Endowment for the Arts.

(Acknowledgments continue on last page of book.)

*In memory of my father
who never gave up the idea
that his country
would one day be free*

VIRGILIO RAFAEL SUÁREZ

1933-1997

Other Works by Virgil Suárez

Fiction:

The Cutter
Latin Jazz
Havana Thursdays
Going Under
Welcome to the Oasis, a novella & stories

Poetry:

Spared Angola: Memories from a Cuban American Childhood
You Come Singing
Garabato Poems
Amazonia, translation

Anthologies:

Iguana Dreams: New Latino Fiction
Paper Dance: 55 Latino Poets
*Little Havana Blues: A Contemporary
    Cuban-American Literature Anthology*

Contents

Part III: *Destierro*

Someone who's been uprooted, exiled, has no country.
Our country exists only in our memory, but we need
something beyond memory if we're to achieve happiness.
We have no homeland, so we have to invent it
over and over again.

—Reinaldo Arenas

PART

Exilio

The Night Train Called *El Lechero*

My father rode it all over Cuba when he foraged
for the food we needed back in the city, food to survive.

He went on long trips and returned with fruit,
vegetables, always tubers like *yuca* and *boniato* my mother

fried up crispy in the lard of pigs we slaughtered. He
brought home turtles, fish, venison, duck, chickens.

El Lechero, the milk train, traveled the island at night,
when fireflies might easily be mistaken for stars.

Most of all, my father brought stories, stories he told
my mother and me during the Havana blackouts.

People on the move, like him looking, foraging for better
chances for themselves. Soldiers, prisoners on their way

to cut sugar cane, lovers coming to the city to get married.
My father told us the story of a man like him, out to find

something to bring back to his family, a sack of rice he bartered
a pair of rabbits for, and the night rain that soaked through his jute

sack which, unbeknownst to the man, had rotted, and when
the man lifted the sack it split down the center and the rice

spilled down the crowded train steps where he and my father
sat and talked of better days in their youth, and I remember

my father's breath almost blowing out the candles my mother
always put on the table in case of a blackout, and the shine

in my father's eyes as he spoke of that man, like him, on his knees,
scooping rice with cupped hands, pleading with the rain

not to wash away the rice that would nourish his family back home,
not to wash away, like everything else in his life: home, family,

opportunity . . . and my father helps the man gather what little
rice remains, then both men sit there in the silence, dulled by the rocking

train, *El Lechero*, which still travels through the island, where boys
stay awake to listen for its whistle, the clank-clank of its wheels

and in the silence it leaves behind, the sound of men as they plead,
plead with the night's rain not to wash so much of their future away.

Bitterness

My father brings home the blood of horses on his hands,
    his rough, callused, thick-fingered hands; he comes home
from the slaughterhouse where the government places him to kill

old, useless horses that arrive from all over the island. On his hands
    it comes, encrusted and etched into the prints and wrinkles
of his fingers, under his nails, dark with the dirt too, the filth and grime,

the moons of his fingers pinked by its residue, his knuckles skinned
    from the endless work. Sticky and sweet-scented is the blood
of these horses, horses to feed the lions in the new zoo which is moving

from Havana to Lenin's Park near where we live. Dark blood, this blood
    of the horses my father slaughters daily, and loses himself doing so.
I, being a child, ask how many horses it takes to feed a single lion.

This, of course, makes my father laugh. I watch as he scrubs and rinses
    dried blood from his forearms and hands, those hands
that kill the horses, the hands that sever through skin and flesh and crush

through bone because tough is the meat of old horses. Feed for the lions.
    So my father, the dissident, the *gusano*, the Yankee lover, walks
to and from work on tired feet, with an aching body. He no longer talks

to anybody, and less to us, his family. My mother and my grandmother;
    his mother. But they leave him alone, to his moods, for they know
what he is being put through. A test of will. Determination. Salvation

and survival. My father, gloomy, under the new zoo tent on the grounds,
    doesn't say much. He has learned how to speak with his hands.
Sharp are the cuts he makes on the flesh. The horses are shot in the open

fields, a bullet through the head, and are then carted to where my father,
    along with other men, do the butchering. He is thirty (the age
I am now) and tired and when he comes home his hands are numb

from all that chopping and sawing. This takes place in 1969. Years later
    when we are allowed to leave Havana for Madrid, to the cold
winter of Spain, we find ourselves living in a hospice. The three of us

in a small room. (My grandmother died and was buried in Havana.)
Next door lives a man named Izquierdo who wakes
us with phlegmy coughs. From our side of the clapboard walls,

his coughing sounds like thunder. We try to sleep; I try harder
but the coughing seeps through and my father curses under his breath.
I listen to the heat as it tic-tacs through the furnace. My father tries

to make love to my mother. I try now not to listen. The mattress
springs sound like bones crushing. My mother refuses without saying
a word. This is the final time she she does so tonight. My father breaks

the immense and interminable silence,saying, "If you don't, I'll look
for a Spanish woman who will."Silence again, then I think I hear
my mother crying. *"Alguien,"* my father says, meaning someone, "Will want

to, to . . . (fuck him.) And I lay there on my edge of the mattress,
sweat summoned by the heat. My eyes are closed and I listen hard
and then everything stops. This, I think, is a sound like death.

Then my father begins all over again. The room fills with small noises . . .
the cleaver falls and cuts through skin, tears through flesh, crushes
the bone, and then there is blood. All that blood. It emerges and collects

on slaughter tables, the blood of countless horses. Sleep upon me, I see
my father stand by the sink in our Havana house patio. He scrubs
and rinses his hands. The blood whirls and dissolves slowly in the water.

Once again I summon the courage to go ahead and ask him how
much horse meat it takes to appease the hunger of a single lion.

Connivance

In the Havana summers
out of school, out of uniform,
we ran in packs, like dingoes
hunted for & killed birds

that dared perch & preen
on tree branches
on the other side of the trash
dump. We destroyed

both fauna & flora, we flung
rocks at the corner street lights.
During the blackouts we snuck
around & banged on trashcans,

for the ruckus, for the candle
light appearing at the windows,
the ghostly shapes of adults.
We roached around & broke

windows, deflated car tires,
stole all we could get our hands
on. How could we not? Already
outcasts in this too-small place,

scarcely heaven, scarcely
ever enough. We pulled
pranks, snuck up on people
in the dark of their porches

& howled like wolves.
Nobody paid much attention.
It was a strange time
for everyone & nobody cared

what we did. Our cousins came
from the provinces & we spied
on them, the girl cousins
while they bathed. We tied

a shard of broken mirror
to the end of a broom stick
& we peeped at them through
an open bathroom window.

Amazed by the tufts of black
hair between their legs,
the prominence of flesh
on their chests. We darted

out of our own backyards
& shouted, full
of bravado & courage,
this was the summer of 1969,

there were countries at war,
people dying everywhere
& we ran, ran to spare ourselves
these limitations in our lives.

The Hatchery

Once in Havana as school children we took a field trip
to a chicken hatchery not too far from the school.

We walked there single file, already a string of blemished
pearls strung by our sweaty hands, divided every

tenth by a teacher. We wore our Young Pioneer uniforms
and the sweat made our shirts stick to our backs, the half

moons wet under our armpits. We walked through chambers
in the hatchery in awe of so much stainless steel, tiled

walls and granite floors, aluminum doors, walked silent
under the flicker of bad fluorescent lights. We got the tour:

eggs on the conveyor belts about to be cleaned of shit,
the sexing tables through which light passed in the eggs,

the incubator room with all the trays from the hatching room.
We walked through single file, passed rooms filled with the chirp

of thousands of baby chicks, a floor gone furry with the downy
white-yellow of baby chicks. The worker/guide explains

the process from fertile eggs to birth. In another room,
a collection of jars with all of nature's anomalies,

"left turns," as the man calls these little accidents. The specimens
float in formaldehyde, aliens from other worlds, we say.

The males, it is explained to us, the few born, are gathered
and separated and fed for only a few days, then they are sent

next door to the grinders. The world goes white and still
when the guide says "*moledoras.*" The teachers look at the guide,

eyes wide open, a sigh on their lips, as if to stop him from going
on about this horrible fate of male chicks in the world of poultry.

What happens there? The male chicks are ground up and mixed
with byproducts to make pellets for farm animals.

We shiver at the news. Later, we each receive a chick to take
home, a science project of our own. Responsibility tests.

We thought of the possibilities, if the chicks we carried close
would grow to be roosters, or grow at all. No matter

for if they did grow, they undoubtedly would end up in the soup.
So many of us walked home that afternoon with our prizes,

some of us giddy with the idea of feeding and nurturing.
Our parents, the dissidents, who wanted no part of the Revolution,

would know what to do with such a precious gift. We held
our chicks close to our hearts, and this memory of our visit

to the hatchery in Havana lingers, the yellow puffs scattered
on the floor like dandelions, free to float in the air at last,

free to float away in the faint breeze of memory, across
the barren and ravaged fields we now call our childhoods.

The Dirt Eaters

Whenever we grew tired and bored of curb ball,
   of encircling the scorpions we found under rocks

by the mother-in-law tongues within a fiery circle
   of kerosene, and watched as they stung themselves

to death, we ate dirt: soft, grainy, pretend-chocolate
   dirt, in our fantasies sent to us by distant relatives

in *El Norte*. *Fango*. We stood in a circle, wet the dirt
   under our bare feet, worked with our fingers to crumble

the clods with our nails, removed the undesired twigs,
   pebbles, and beetles. Dirt—how delicious. How filling.

We ate our share of it back then. Beto, the youngest,
   warned us not to eat too much, it could make us sick,

give us the shits, vomit, or even worse, worms.
   We laughed. We ridiculed him. We chanted

after him: "*¡Lo que no mata, engorda!*
   ¡Lo que no mata, engorda!"

What doesn't kill you makes you fat and stronger.

Pox

the neighbors called it *viruela*,
    for chicken pox. *La China,*
rubiola, different names
    for the same thing: skin
eruptions that as a child
    broke the skin, globules
of pus against flannel
    pajamas dried
overnight, stuck
    against the fabric.
The first morning
    my mother took off
my shirt, I felt the scabs
    rip skin. Blood
seeped down my arms
    and the sides of my rib
cage, down my back,
    then my mother found
a better method. She bathed
    me in the tub with hydrogen
peroxide to loosen the grasp
    of dried-up pus against skin,
and ward off infection, too,
    and it worked. The malaise
passed, and then all that was left
    were these red dots
on my skin, a map of them,
    you could connect them
and know the meaning,
    a Braille history of pain . . .
the rubric of memory,
    lexicon of pockmarked skin.

Las Tendederas / **Clotheslines**

The day my mother stood in the kitchen
    & cooked all the turtle meat from the turtles
        I helped my father kill & she screamed

when the sizzling chunks started to jump
    & we rushed in to check on what was up
        & my father told her that it was okay,

that turtle meat always did that when fried
    & then we got back to the slaughter of the pig
        my father had bartered a dozen rabbits for

& when we finally cornered it at the end
    of the walkway by the side of the house,
        next to the chicken coop, it squealed & set

the chickens all aflutter & a cloud of dust
    rose, a combination of dirt & dung
        & my father got something in his eyes

& he laughed & I sneezed & sneezed
    & when the chickens settled down the pig
        snuck by us & ran back to the patio,

knocking on its way the stick holding up
    my mother's clothesline & all the laundry
        drying fell on the dirt & the pig trampled

it & it made my father so angry he took
    the wire from the clothesline, looped it over
        the pig's neck & when the pig stood still

my father reeled it in & with a broom handle
    he applied a tourniquet to the pig
        & with a final squeal it dropped on its front

knees, choked by the wire which cut so deep
blood spurted onto everything, mainly
my mother's washed clothes; the pig stood

still long enough for my father to plunge
a knife into its heart. There we stood, my
father & I, out of breath, he with bloodied

arms & myself with the pangs of excitement
loose in my chest. Amazed by the slaughter
of so many animals in one afternoon, I stood

there quiet, caught in the splendor of my mother's
once-white laundry. My father put the clothesline
back & one by one I picked all the garments

from the ground & carried them to my mother.
With a cigarette in his mouth, my father leaned
against the door frame, a satisfied look on his face,

a smile on his lips. This was Havana in 1968
& I have never seen my father more content.
Now when I travel the open roads of the U.S.,

I look across the expanse of peoples' yards
& when I see clotheslines, laundry-heavy & bowed,
swaying in the breeze & the fact that someone

worked so hard at putting it up & out, I think
about how much debris time & distance
have kicked up into my eyes.

The Parable of Stones

once the rock struck
between the eyes, I saw

it come but didn't duck
behind the palm tree in time—

I felt pain blind the eyes,
the trickle of blood down

the cheek, then lightness
of the head, a spinning world.

Then I was flat on my back
looking up at the faces of friends,

among them the culprit
who'd flung the rock—in his eyes

the fact that both blood and stone
had become one: a weight

too heavy for the both of us
to carry our entire lives.

Luz & Balmaseda Street Corner Games

There was *quimbumbia* where we placed one stick
on top of another, like in a cross, then we hit

the stick and watched it soar. Stickball we played
with a broomstick and balled-up newspaper

bound tight with string and tape. Dagger
was played with an ice pick which we tossed

high in the sky and watched for where/how
it landed. Curb ball when we got lucky

and someone got a rubber ball for *Los Reyes.*
Marbles when we found ball bearings or used

smooth, pretty round pebbles. *Caracoles,* or snail
shells: the objective was to knock one against

the other, first shell to cave in lost. When it rained
we made wooden boats and raced them in the muddy

currents that ran down the street. Our fathers made
papalotes, kites, out of bamboo and rice paper,

with long strips of old bed sheets as tails. We put razor
blades on them or tied on a broken piece of bottle and fought

air wars. Those of us with relatives in the United States,
the lucky few, received balloons and gum in letters

sent to our parents. The balloons didn't last and the gum,
too sweet, made us sick. On the way home one day,

I looked down at the sidewalk and found what I thought
was a balloon, but it turned out to be a used condom.

When my father saw me with it in my mouth
as I tried to inflate it, all color bled from his cheeks.

He came after me, grabbed the thing out of my mouth,
and threw it away. He couldn't tell me what it was I had

done wrong. How could he begin to explain?
When the games came to an end because by 1969

none of us got toys, or the relatives stopped sending
these small gifts, and our imaginations ebbed dry,

we resorted to flinging rocks at the street lights.
We broke them so many, so many times, the city refused

to replace them. And after that, we built
darts out of chicken feathers, sticks, and needles.

We threw them at each other. Those, too, were taken
away. Everything was confiscated, either by parents

or government. The last *Navidades* and *Reyes Magos*
I spend in Cuba, my father got in line for four days

and three nights. When his number came up, there was one
last bicycle, which he bought and brought home, so proud.

To his son. And what did I do? I took the wheels
apart, removed the inner tube, and made the best slingshot

anybody in the neighborhood had seen. Even after the beating
I got from both my mother and father, I became the talk

of the schoolyard, the talk of the neighborhood. Everyone
agreed I was a crazy bastard, with the best slingshot

anybody had ever laid eyes on. No one knocked
out more street lights than I did. No one shot down more birds.

No one, for that entire year, wanted to be a better friend to me.
For an only child, what better way to learn the meaning of fickle?

Excerpt from the Book of Hollows

One summer in my Cuban childhood
   my paternal grandfather took me
on horseback to check many of the water

wells in the countryside of San Pablo.
   We rode out before the midday heat,
when the scent of melons and squash

drying against scorched earth hung heavy
   and thick in the air. It was a summer
of drought and my grandfather spoke

of water wells where the water
   to keep the cattle and other animals
alive came from. The first we checked

was next to the henhouse in the shade
   of a blooming guayaba. A wide
oval-shaped opening in the ground,

only covered by sheets of corrugated
   metal and planks of wood, holes
rusted through, shafts of sunlight

plunging into the dark of the well,
   motes and dust adrift in the air.
Growing up here, all my cousins

and I heard stories of the people
   who'd fallen into these deep wells,
never to be heard from or rescued.

My grandfather checked for water levels
   by dropping a wood bucket or gourd
down beyond where the sunlight shone,

way down in the darkness where,
    after many feet of rope, the thud
and splash of the bucket echoed

like something calling, a ghost of the fallen.
    We were told of the things these wells
claimed, mostly animals like goats,

chickens, a fox, and children, who didn't
    didn't listen always to adults.
And as my grandfather and I traveled

and checked all the wells, I thought
    of these depths, these hollows
of ground and how, if you put your ear

close to the dry earth, you could hear faint
    voices of those who'd succumbed
to the charmed calling of such dark depths.

San Lázaro's Procession

It started at dusk or early that morning
in Havana (or was it dusk?) by the time
devotees moved through our neighborhood,

many dressed in white, those on their knees
already bloody and scarred, others sunken
into their crutches, the absence of limb

obvious, pant leg folded and tucked
at the knee. All broken, damaged somehow
in this life, intent on kept promises. All

on their way to *El Rincón* de San Lázaro,
up on the hill, so far from where these people
had started their pilgrimages, to see

that old leper in loin cloth, surrounded
by his three faithful dogs which lick
and heal his festering wounds, the saint

the Catholic church doesn't recognize,
says is only myth, but what about these
believers, moving through on pure will?

My parents brought me to the side of the street
where people in Calabazar stood
and watched the procession of the sick

and infirm, not unlike the rest of us,
penitent of sins, expectant that a kept promise
could set them on the right path to freedom.

I was never taken to the place where they say
people left their offerings: casts, crutches,
hair, medicines for bad hearts, bad teeth,

flowers—left there at the altar by people
who claimed some certain healing took place
in their lives, and they merely walked away,

healed, new. I was a child in the awe
of such searches of spirit to a Cuban saint
whose charm I would never understand,

but so many, unlike me, so lifted by faith
and trust, moved by their beliefs, came through
so much hardship, determined in their passing—

bent on this idea left to them, they made
the journey to the little hilltop sanctuary
in the dark of their land, of my childhood.

So many people passed to leave some mark,
some token, like this poem, an amulet left
as a gift in the shrine of such yearning.

Papalotes / Kites

Next door to El Volcán *bodega*
run by El Chino Chan, my father
bought the kites made by Chan's
brother, a man without a name,

without a country, who made kites
by the hundreds and hung them
from the rafters of the ceiling
of his kite shop. Rumor had it,

the man fled China young
to avoid Mao's communism.
He supposedly was a great painter
back in his country, but here

in Havana, he made kites,
these hexagonal-shaped kites
made of rice paper, which cost
up to five pesos or higher

depending on the size, color,
shape, and front painting.
I visited the shop a couple
of times with my father

who sometimes didn't want
to spend the money
on the *papalotes* I chose.
I chose them fast, because

they were all fine, amazing
rather, breathtaking in color.
I liked the ones with the dragon
heads painted on them,

fire-breathing, wide-eyed,
gold- and silver-scaled,
but what I liked best
was to be able to inch my way

closer to the table where Chan's
brother worked, surrounded
by the paints, inks, ribbons,
thin colored papers he cut out

from, the smell of the starch
glue he kept warm by the table,
the spools of string, everything
there. Chan's brother kept

his distance, didn't appreciate
the scrutiny. If you got too close,
he would tap you on the head with a ruler.
He drank tea, the steam rose into

his chestnut-colored eyes
and made them look sad, moist
as though he was always crying.
His hair was always combed

and oiled. He sat at his table
and drew this in continuous lines:
egrets by a river's edge, a tiger
about to leap, a fighting rooster.

Then, one day the shop closed
and never reopened. Chan's
brother disappeared. Who
knew what happened? Chan

couldn't say. For days it is said
Chan didn't speak, and when
he did it was only to complain
of his slow and nosy customers.

Rumor had it Chan's brother
had left for the United States.
You could still see all the kites,
everything where the man left them.

Me, I had a couple of magnificent
kites, ones called *generales*
& *comandantes*. Big, tall,
the kind that when you flew

them tugged at you
much like a current,
a hard undertow
like this memory now

of Chan's brother
and his wonderful kites.

Urchins

In the Havana of my childhood, when I was six,
    my father took me by bus to the beach.
My mother packed us a travel bag with our towels,

some sandwiches, crackers with homemade
    mango jam, a change of clothes. We rode
the packed diesel bus, he holding on to my hand,

saying: *lata de sardinas*; me pressed against the bodies
    of strangers—a little dizzy from the fuel fumes
and the stop & go, stop & go, and each time we made

it there early enough so that the beach seemed less crowded,
    smooth white sand already hot underfoot, Santa María,
Miramar now called Patricio Lumumbe

after the African martyr. My father taught me to swim
    there, he'd hold me flat against the surface
of the water, saying: "*¡Patalea! Usa los brazos, las manos.*"

Use my arms, my hands. Kick. Slowly I got the hang
    of it and I floated, buoyant in the salt and sun,
even though a couple of times I swallowed water

through my nose. Braver, I learned to dunk my head under,
    pinch my nose shut, keep my eyes closed.
To this day, I still do that. My father taught me how

to dive off the crab-infested jetty rocks. Then one day
    another kid loaned me a scuba mask and I looked
under the water for the first time, and I saw them, urchins,

scattered on the bottom, like some lost treasure spilled
    from a chest, moving only with the tug
and ebb of the tides, prickly in their armor. Some red,

others black, and my father warned me not to step
   on one, that it'd hurt like hell to get one of those spikes
in my foot, so I kept my distance. Saw polka-dotted damsel

fish, the red-green parrot wrasse—of course, I didn't know
   the names of any of these creatures back then,
but I loved the way they swam next to me. Once,

a nurse shark swam by and I reached out to touch
   its skin, and it felt rough, gritty like everything else
on that beach. My father would lie on the sand to catch

some sun; I waded in the surf not too far from him,
   the sun warming the skin on my forehead and shoulders.
My mother has pictures of those days, the skinny kid

leaning against his tall father, of that beach, of the shimmering
   surface of the water, and out on the horizon the barges
I learned later were filled with urchins, thousands of them,

dragged out, exposed, dying in the sun, much like what would
   happen to us in our own country, those of us called
gusanos, the dissidents, those who quickly learned to live with exile,

in exile, for another forty years. I look at that picture
   of the urchin slaughter and my eyes burn,
burn because I understand what it means to be away from water.

Cochino

was what they called us,
the children of dissidents,
    the *gusanos*: Pigs, swine.

Cochinitos when we picked
    our noses in mixed company
or soiled our underwear.

    The diminutive is sweeter
sounding. *Puerco*, if we
    did something disgusting,

like throw up because
    we often gagged on the bad
food the Revolution provided.

    They said you Catholic pigs
pray for food and we'd pray,
    yet out of the cafeteria

nothing came. Its swinging
    doors still on their hinges,
then they told us to ask Fidel

    and the Revolution for our daily
bread, and we shouted
    and the food appeared in carts.

We learned to accept this new
    label—hunger knows no dignity.
We sat and ate as quickly as we dared.

    Now, all that past, twenty-five
years ago, and we still gather
    from Miami to Los Angeles,

Christmas Eve, United States,
    the ritual of the open pit
on the ground, pig roasting.

    We slaughter, we roast,
the drippings sizzle, our
    hearts grow content, tender,

at the thought that we've made
    it through another year of exile.
So we open another beer,

    take a cool swig, taste the crunchy
and delicious crispy skins.
    Good stuff. On the stereo

the music of Cuba long ago.
    Pork rinds, sweet and tasty,
some say we've come so far

    to eat so well. We savor
all the meanings in the flesh
    of this beast called *cochino*.

Epidemic

During my last Havana summer,
    an epidemic broke out all over the island,
some German virus that started

first in pigs, then infected humans
    in those nether regions—who knew
if they existed, where animals subsisted

with humans. No one knew if the rumor
    of such a disease was true. But one
day the Russian-built army trucks

arrived, the gravel crunched under
    such weight through our neighborhood,
the armed soldiers spilled out canvas-

tarped backs like grain from a sack,
    and the bulldozers came and dug
huge pits at the corner clearing

where people threw trash, left
    brujería-sacrificed animals, then while
more pits were being dug, the soldiers

marched down the streets, house
    by house, confiscated all the animals
in people's patios and yards, one by one,

especially the pigs which squealed
    like it was the end of the world, and it was.
They came and took our six-month piglet.

Our Christmas food. Our rabbits, chickens,
    even the pet turtle in the cement sink.
All the animals herded toward the corner,

in Noah's ark fashion, to the edge
        of the pit where they stopped and fought
back the precipice. Men with blowtorches

set them afire, shot the larger animals
        like horses and cows and pigs, torched
the smaller ones, chicken and duck

feathers burned in midair. We gathered
        at the corner, too afraid of perhaps being
next. We children stood by our parents

and watched as the animals fell, carcasses
        charred and burnt to cinders, charred dominos
atop each other. The fires burned for a couple

of days and for weeks later, flecks of ashes
        fell over everything, the smell of flesh, offal,
and hide thick in the air. Even now, from

the distance of thirty years, I can hear the pop
        and sizzle of fur burning, the talk of fire, how
everything was taken away, except

for this burning that lingers in the mind,
        some torch of resentment, blackness
of remembrance that refuses to be doused.

Lenin's Park, Havana

built for tourism, mainly to show
how the Revolution had triumphed—

an amphitheater, roller coasters,
a place to house the country's fairs,

fine restaurants, a convention center.
On opening day all of Havana came

to witness the glory. The army
demonstrated its might by parachuting

men from planes, the tanks rolled
in, soldiers on horseback—the children

received free chocolate bars and ice cream,
cotton candy, the adults free shots of coffee.

The Havana zoo moved here and opened
the same day, free passes for everyone.

The whole park offered much, mainly
employment for the citizens, a place

to go to when boredom hit, and for us,
the children of Arroyo Naranjo, the place

became our new playground, our church.
We balanced on the train rails,

we ran and skipped the tiles, placed bottle
caps to be flattened by the passing train,

hunted for birds, lizards, bugs, anything
we could get our hands on. We built

traps, played cowboys and Indians,
and at school they taught us about the name

of the park, the significance of what one man
can accomplish for his own country, like Fidel,

like Che, like Camilo—and for those of us,
the *gusanos*, the dissidents, we saw

our parents go off into the fields to cut
sugar cane, to work "voluntarily."

Our fathers, some, went off to the prisons
because of accusations, for not wanting

to leave their families for the sugar cane fields.
My own father worked at the zoo, slaughtered

horses to feed the big cats and crocodiles.
To us the world had changed, it changed

every day. At school, we learned the impact
of a man who loaned our little island, our city

a park a year after it was built we couldn't go to,
we couldn't even pay to get in because we no

longer belonged, no longer existed, and so we
snuck in and played, played like the ghosts

our parents, our families, our selves had become,
and people said that at night they could see us,

they could hear us, the chants, the prayers,
the flashing of our lives, like fireflies,

sending signals, clues that one day our parents
would take us away to some other country,

some other place where we'd learn some new
history, and the true meaning of what yearns to be free.

What We Took

when we left Havana
in December of 1970:

nothing but coats
my father bartered

rabbits and chickens for,
my mother reinforced

their itchy wool linings,
the best shoes we owned,

scarves my mother knitted,
gloves which she cut

from patterns traced
by penciling the outline

of our hands, photos
of my grandparents,

uncles, aunts, cousins,
my mother's younger brother

Ovidio, who posed in military
uniform, the airport guard

confiscated the picture,
State property, he argued,

no jewelry, no other items
of clothing, personal possessions.

When we arrived in Madrid,
people looked at us, askance

stares, as uncomfortable as ours,
as though we were a trio

of rare birds (desert penguins?)
In these costumes, mementos

of our difficult, dark passage
like badges of our exiled lives.

Wake

The day somebody died in the neighborhood
    Manuel sent Ricardito, his son,
to go to the wake with his mother.

Ricardito, no older than eight,
    heard his father tell his mother
about making sure to offer the bereaved

family sympathy, *El pésame*, he called it,
    Spanish for condolences, and so when
the time came he watched as people approached

the open casket and knelt, Ricardito took
    his turn but couldn't take his eyes
away from the lips of the deceased, the way

bad light made them ruby, the way one nostril
    seemed more open then the other,
and the single thick hair that protruded

from a narrow nostril. He knelt there
    and told the deceased how sorry
he was. He offered the dead

man his sympathy, something he knew
    nothing about. He had seen the life
flash out of a little sparrow's eyes when he

shot it from the clothesline with a sling
    shot he'd built from surgical tubing,
but though he thought of the word *dolor*,

he came up empty. When he and his mother
    returned home, Manuel asked how
everything went and Ricardito told him

what he said, the words he'd spoken
        to the dead man, and his father couldn't
control his laughter at his son making such

an innocent mistake. "What did he say to you?"
        Manuel asked his son, who stood confused,
more distraught than ever. "Nothing," he answered.

"He lay there in the box, not saying anything."
        Ricardito stood in the living room
and smiled when his parents chuckled and laughed.

He wondered if these two same adults would laugh
        if he told them that the deceased had spoken
to him, in the way the dead man puckered his lips

into a bright and beautiful rose which contained
        all this nervous adult laughter of the living.

PART

Refugio

In the Land of Earthquakes

When my parents and I first arrived in Los Angeles,
we all slept badly. Together in the only room with a bed,

we tossed and turned, enveloped in the same bad dreams,
the weight of the thousands of miles we'd traveled

still heavy on our bodies: Havana, Madrid, Miami . . .
My mother heard about the earthquakes in California

on the radio at work. One night when we had our first
television set, we watched footage of the 1906 San Francisco

quake. The way they come unannounced—only dogs
detect the change in the air, those rhythms deep under

ground, so she kept asking my father to bring home
a small dog, just to be safe. She took to buying supplies:

soap, bottled water, flashlights and batteries. The drawers
filled with them. At night when the rumbling started,

she woke up, woke us up, my father and I, in a sweat,
and she said, half asleep, "This is it. This is the big one."

My father, eyes sealed with the day's hard work, rolled over
and muttered: "It's only the train passing by. That's it."

I slept in the hollows of their bodies, these concaves of soft
flesh, a child already ridden with too many adultlike fears.

"Next time for sure," my mother said and held me tight.

Oneida

my mother comes from the land of tropical fruit,
    of red clay and the oxen cart.

At an early age she learned to brew coffee
    through a sock, wash & clean rice,

wring the necks of chickens, of guinea fowl.
    The youngest in a family of eight,

she learned to make do. In 1961, she married
    her policeman sweetheart, a man resigned

to crisp uniforms, boots, and the shine of smooth
    cuticles. Soon everything in her life

would change forever. A child, a house, a country
    of scarcity and invention—*El Destino*.

She followed my father to Spain, leaving her land,
    her people—forever, she knew. It took guts,

no doubt. More than have been passed down to me
    in the genes. In Los Angeles, California,

she worked in the sweatshop factories, piecemeal
    seamstress work. Ten years later,

it was still time measured at ten cents per piece,
    the faster she sewed, the more she made,

and brought this gift of money earned with callused
    hands home to her family, in this new country

of possibilities, having come from the land of rain—
    all that water . . . and fear of the big

earthquake. She learned to drive, to make friendships,
    the stop and go, stop and start. No time

for roots. A widow now, so many miles from home,
    native or exiled, she is a woman born again,

dignified, a woman who's learned the trick
    of desire's fire as she constantly rises

from the smoldering embers of this place,
    in solitude, she's learned to call home.

Free

When we first arrived in the United States
from Franco's Spain, everything we encountered

or bought had "free" written on it.
The boxes of cereal spoke of a free mystery

surprise, the junk mail came bundled
and somehow that word sang to us.

My father and I got wise—the word
became cheap, untrustworthy, hollow.

Having been fooled before, we knew what "free"
really meant. We learned lessons the hard way,

nothing free ever came so easily, but my mother,
who had heard stories of people throwing

out televisions sets, sofas, washing machines,
perfectly good chairs—believed in this land

of plenty where people discarded simply
because things were old or someone

had grown tired of them. She believed
in all that was cast to the curb. A cousin

who cruised the neighborhood streets
for these free goods told her of his finds

over the telephone. On the weekends,
she sent my father and me out to hunt,

to find these throwaways, but we always
came back empty-handed. We never

really looked. We stopped for donuts
or to watch a baseball game at the park.

Now, years later, my father dead, my mother
gets the mail, the catalogues, and she sends

it all up to me in Tallahassee, and she's circled
the word "free" and asks me what the deal is.

Most Sundays I try to convince her once
and for all that there are no deals, that nothing

is free, then there's silence over the line
and I can hear her thinking otherwise.

She is a woman who wants to cling to something
as simple as a two-for-one deal, the extra, the much

more, the free: these simple things she knows
have kept us going all these exiled years.

El Refugio / Freedom Tower, Miami, Florida

My father, a proud man, boasted that our family never needed it

to get our feet on the ground, so to speak, when we first arrived

in the United States from Cuba. Actually we came via Madrid, Spain,

where we also didn't need to go to El Comedor, a soup kitchen cafeteria

where exiled Cubans gathered to look for work or pass time.

Many of the family's friends did stay at El Refugio in Miami where

they ate, slept, waited for news of work and/or more arriving family.

Where so many quickly grew tired of the daily fried slab of Spam

sandwiches, croquettes, the watery coffee and powdered milk,

the second-hand clothes, the constant smoking in the hallways,

the interminable peering southward to that island ninety miles

in the distance, the blinding distance, invisible now, unattainable

forever. Someone recites lines from José Martí: "*Las playas del*

destierro no son . . ." Many remember El Refugio as the place where

they were told that freedom meant getting a job first. Many looked

for and waited for a man they came to know as "Yeyo Pages," he who

could get them work in the Yellow Pages. Or were told to go by the stores

where the "Sale" signs hung behind windows. Sale in Spanish

means "to exit" and the Cuban refugees knew the word with great

intimacy but when they heard "Sale" they thought of the miracle of

language: "*Tú entras y te va bien, todo bien barato.*" My father always sat

and listened to these stories about El Refugio, the Freedom Tower, and he

often smiled and the pride showed in his eyes and he'd say to people:

"*Ni* El Refugio. *Ni el* Welfare." We didn't need either. In Miami, they

have refurbished and painted this building, at one time the tallest in

the city, on Biscayne Blvd., now a landmark much like Ellis Island

where so many came, saw, changed their names, learned to live with

the fire of longing raging deep in the heart.

New Toothpaste

Showered, my wife stands at the sink
    and brushes her teeth. I hear her
hum, then she rinses and says, "Gritty."
"What is?" I ask. The new tooth-
paste, the one with baking soda
    for tartar control and what they
pass as "fresh," sandy, tri-colored
    in its gelled form, and I think
of my father who, having arrived
    in the U.S. from Cuba, the land
of his youth and scarcity, collected
    toothpaste. I can't imagine
what toothpaste fulfilled in his world
    of lack, but he bought half
a dozen tubes weekly, every time
    he went to the market.
He bought different brands,
    even the ones he grew allergic
to, the ones with peroxide.

When we visited my parents, my wife
    who didn't believe me about
my father's hoarding, bent to look
    at the stacks in the bathroom
cabinet. We used the toothpaste
    he bought. Each tube
had its own squeeze-the-last-drop
    contraption. We also saw
a couple of tubes slit down the center
    like the carcass of some animal,
gutted and emptied. Amazed each time
    I'd approach my father

and remind him we lived in the U.S.A.
   With a satisfied look on his face,
he'd say that toothpaste would not let him
   forget about what I now take
for granted, this basic difference between us,
   father and son, how toothpaste
reminds us all of how far we've traveled.

Lily

was our next-door neighbor on Palm Street
in Bell, California. She lived alone after

her husband died, years before we moved
in next door. Every morning, she worked

her tomato garden until noon, stood
straight to say goodbye when we left

for work or school. She spoke choppy
Spanish to my mother, said she wanted

to be neighborly. To me, she handed
the basketball when it went over

the fence into her yard. She gave us
tomatoes, chili peppers—all varieties.

She said she loved Mexican food,
not realizing we were not Mexicans.

She lived alone; at night she left many
lights on in the house. I saw

her drift like a ghost from room to room.
At night when I couldn't sleep, I caught

glimpses of Lily reading the newspaper,
knitting a sweater, turning her face away

as though she were talking to someone.
I knew she lived alone. She once told

me her daughters, all grown, lived
in another state, flight attendants or CEOs

or something, too busy to visit.
Lily lived on inside her house,

out in her garden. My parents took her
food made with vegetables she had given us.

There was great sadness in Lily's eyes,
and my mother said it was too hard

to visit Lily, her rough Spanish,
and my mother's nonexistent English,

but they communicated as best as possible,
a language of recognition for hard work,

work well done, and when Lily went away,
the "For Sale" sign staked into her lawn,

this whole corner seemed to sag a little,
a chick sparrow flung from its nest,

we knew what this emptiness meant,
we watched as weeds ravaged her garden,

we lived on through the night, Lily's house
dark, abandoned, like a "wolf's mouth,"

my father said. Goodbye and good luck,
I whispered against the window glass,

the condensation of my breath
like some screen against something cruel.

Tío Hipólito

my mother's great uncle
      who arrives from Cuba,
for a first & last visit to Miami.

We pick him up at the hustle-push
      airport. He is a man
of scarcity, from a land leached

of time. He doesn't know much
      about planes, designer
jeans, CPUs, slurpees.

The minute he climbs in the Volvo
      for our trip home,
he weeps. He doesn't feel well.

He tells us about his dead son,
      at forty-five still a young man,
who died a year ago

of a massive coronary in the shower.
      We learn all this between sobs.
Not fair, he says, *for my son to die before me.*

He used to believe in a higher being.
      Miracles. Who can believe
when so much is taken away? Country,

wife, son—nothing is left but
      this man, this angel from paradise
dressed in a cloud-colored overcoat

in 90-degree Miami weather,
      being driven to a strange place,
by a stranger who'd like

to trade eyes for his, what
      he's seen, for the miles his shoes
have traveled, grand beneath them.

Piedad

She named her only son, her only blood link

      Guantánamo, named after the Bay,

conceived with an American Marine, olive-skinned,

      green-eyed, in 1959, the eve of the Revolution,

when all she wanted was the freedom to learn law.

      She longed to be the best attorney, but things

changed, things always change for her, when she

      closes her eyes and concentrates on the warm hum

of her thoughts taking flight, like the Fokker plane

      which brought them to this new land.

Now in the city of Nuestra Señora de Los Ángeles,

      she and Guantánamo live in an efficiency—it's all

he can afford. Guantánamo cashiers at Los Dos Toros

      Supermarket where the Mexican stock boys call

her son La Reina, La Mera Mera Cubanita. They

      also call him *joto, puto, maricón*, and Guantánamo

ignores them. She knows all about her son's difference.

      She knew when he was five and she saw him in her

only satin slip, her slippers on, lipstick on his lips.

      Sometimes at night she holds her son when he cries,

a passion like the one she has for Octavio Paz,

      the great Mexican poet to whom she's built

an altar on top of the refrigerator, along with Santa

       Bárbara, the patron saint of The Crossing.

She knows his work by heart. Often when he reads

       an essay on the KMEX station, she leans back into

the softness of the worn sofa and closes her eyes.

       "Between now and now, between I am and you are

the word *bridge*," reads the great poet from his book

       Salamandra, a poem titled "The Bridge." Her crossing:

Ninety miles of water. Her distant childhood. A land

       of potential. Now, here, Guantánamo lives with her,

shares the solitude and silence of her days. Then one

       day, Guantánamo calls her to come and pick out

the mangos and avocados she will need for salad.

       While at the market, two men storm in and shoot

the butcher and Papito, the owner, and hold the gun

       behind her son's head. *The money*, they shout.

She drops the fruit and runs to her son, the blood that calls.

       The robber, spooked, puts a bullet through Guantánamo's

head and he sags to the dirty linoleum. She holds him

       while he bleeds to death, his father's green eyes water,

and she holds on, holds him to her bosom, this life given,

       this life taken, a woman who cannot settle for much less.

San Luis, Gardener of Miniature Roses

God knows I've tried
to grow some here
in Tallahassee, like yours,

not a blemish or wilt,
each bud a perfect world,
the way you did on Ever-

green Street, South Gate, CA,
but it's not a matter
of the green thumb, know-how,

of the right fertilizer,
organic or non
of watering

of weeding
of keeping snails
out of the beds,

of the right dirt mixture.
No, it takes your hands,
the years you sat on the porch rocker

singing & talking of long-gone days
in your fertile homeland,
of the smooth, green touch

of your breath,
kisses on the petals.
Only then can you witness

the plants' growth,
the unfolding of buds into flower,
like the gift of your hands,

a love for the simple pleasures
we try desperately
to grow. Nourish.

The Seamstress

When she thinks of what is the one constant
    in her life, she thinks of the stitch. The way
the needle punctures cloth and sets

the thread. She remembers when she saw
    the Singer machine at her grandmother's
house, the woman with the cloudy eyes,

the black-gap mouth, the woman who
    told stories of witches by the bridge,
of specters by the side of country roads

who suckled on the blood of humans, of serpents
    who swallowed sugar cane cutters—asleep
under the shade of *framboyanes* and *mameyes*—whole,

the woman whose face appears in the wrinkles
    of the fabric she now sews together. She
loves the hum and vibrations of the machine's

motor, makes stitching a constant clatter
    much like the sound of the women of her childhood
who beat and cleaned rice in the hot morning

sun. She is alone now, the mother of a child
    grown and gone from her home, married with
children of his own. She is here in Hialeah,

alone in the three-bedroom apartment her late
    husband, three months in the grave, worked
alongside her so hard for. They came to Los

Angeles in 1974, and from that beginning
    the constant she depended on was the sound
of an overlap machine stitching zippers to denim

pants, piecemeal, piecemeal—the pay never
        going higher than ten cents per piece. What comfort
is the sound of this machine her husband bought

for her. He knew what sewing means to her,
        the kind of disappearance she relishes in her
childhood. Here she is, a widow, far from her

country of birth, far from her sisters and brothers.
        Her father still alive, her mother in the ground,
and quite suddenly she feels the urge to laugh,

laugh at how time weaves itself into the intricacies
        of the spirit, of the heart; she is planning a return
to the island of her birth, but first she will finish

this dress for her oldest granddaughter, a child
        born in this country, speaking no other language
than the language of her birthplace. What joy

she feels as the lace moves under her fingers,
        the dress almost finished, she will wear it, become
the child in the photos, travel back to her country,

go through the empty rooms of an empty house,
        feel the heat of her birthplace, hear the cries
of a child about to be born in 1938, San Pablo, Cuba.

Las malas lenguas

was what my parents called gossip,
these ill-founded rumors

like the one that always reached us
in Los Angeles, that Cuba was free,

that Castro had cancer of the lungs,
was dying of swollen glands,

brain tumors, heart attacks, *la bola*,
as it is known. These tales zoom

from Miami to Los Angeles, the weekly
express, these speculations all Cubans

hope are true: Muhammad Ali in Havana,
Jesse Jackson, Ted Turner, all calling

for the end of the embargo, none
saying how the revolution

failed its people. Send medicine,
send food, send *dólares*—the island,

El Cocodrilo, stretching against the pull
of so much burden, dives under to cleanse

itself in the Caribbean waters,
and when it surfaces it emerges anew,

virgin forests, new skin, untrampled
streets, fields fertile again . . . we like to believe

in how the heart manages to fool us,
though instinct tells us otherwise,

Las malas lenguas here, there, everywhere.

My Cuban Parents Learn
English in Night School

to, two, too
there, their, they're

two to tango
factory work

yeses & noses
picky bosses

piecemeal work
conjunctions, verbs,

prepositions
"C" is for Capitalism,

compounds of colors:
fuchsia, ambrosia

ochre hearth
flies in the buttermilk

shoofly's shoes
cheaper, faster

hocus-pocus
faster, cheaper

heebie-jeebies
everyday of the week

repeat after me
hard work, hard work

crows the raven:
speak English

The Cubanito All-Stars

our pee-wee baseball
league team. Our fathers

signed us up to play,
they thought we'd be crucial

to the team, then disappointment
set in, we couldn't play infield,

or outfield where the balls went up
so high we lost them in the sky,

then they fell right next
to us, and we'd pick them up

like broken fingers and threw them
toward home plate, more dropped balls.

We grew tired of kicking our heels
into the soggy grass,

of pulling clumps with dirt,
of spitting into the gopher holes,

and balls rained down as we lost
game after game after game,

long after our fathers
left the bleachers, their absence

these gaps of emptiness.
In the cold our breath smoked

in front of our faces: hey, batter!
another gasp to loss of innocence.

Rehab

all skin & bones,
my father is too thin,
taut flesh,
welted veins on his temples
ramifications
down his face, eyes, nose, mouth

here sits the man
who harassed me as a child,
teenager, & not so long
ago refused to speak
to me because I wore my hair
shoulder length

not good enough for him,
who'd worn his 50's
Cuban police crewcut,
he listens to exile radio
propaganda stations
of crazy notions & ideas

about people he knows next
to nothing about,
nothing to do & all the time
not to get it done
orders & reads
all the junk mail

& catalogues,
goes out for walks
around the block, confronts
total strangers who litter,
helps children cross
the street from the school at the corner,

studies for the naturalization
exam, for he yearns
to be a certified
United States citizen
when back in the 60's
when he was being persecuted

for anti-revolutionary
activities, he stood a different
man, once threw a makeshift
kerosene lamp against the wall
& set the house on fire,
he was losing his mind

& the government arrested
him & forced him to work
the sugar cane fields
which nearly cost him his life,
this same man who sat
& watched as my mother

(during my days of drink
& staying out all night)
broke my bottles of wine
in the sink & threw
himself on his knees
& braced my legs

when I threatened to leave
the house for good,
the man whom I helped
while he slaughtered
so many animals, the same
who brought dirty magazines

in the trunk of the '65 Dodge Dart
to my friend's house
driven by some sense of fatherly
duty to expose me to the flesh,
took me to the shops
then embarrassed me because

he argued with the cashiers
who refused to speak
to him in his native Spanish,
& he knew they spoke it,
but he went ahead & bought
the train set for me, the speed car

set, the bicycle, later the Mustang,
he worked two jobs
because he cared,
though he never admitted it,
more about his family
than most men I know,

but the accident changed
all that: 576 pounds
of compressed cardboard
on a pallet fell on him at work,
on my father, the company man,
the lover of eight-to-five jobs,

no questions asked, week in/week out
the weight fell on him & crushed
him, broke his spinal cord
in two places, shattered his skull,
fractured his pelvis into four,
ruptured his testicles, spleen & lower

intestines, took away any semblance
of the man I knew, the man
I know now acts defeated,
has given up, contemplates
the life that could have been,
speaks of exile, of suicide,

of hurling himself from a second story
but the apartment in Hialeah
has bars on the windows,
he knows this is not viable
so he tries to open the passenger
door when I'm driving

but forgets he's buckled
& he cries, curses, shouts
at me, at my mother,
this is not who I was, he screams
this is not who I wanted to be,
my mother caresses his hair

I keep driving & do not look
over to him because I don't
want him to think that I am ashamed
because then he *will* kill himself,
so I reach out
& grab his hand

& tell him what I said
as he lay unconscious in the ICU,
with so many cables going in/out
of him: that it's okay,
he's done good,
hard to convince a man who's lost
his spirit to hang in there.

Break

How much longer, father,
    until the bays of your hairline
        become oceans of skin
            on your forehead? When your hair
        falls & you'll have to wipe

the sweat from your brow
    with a handkerchief—
        more things to carry, to worry about.
        You old immigrant. Refugee.
        Out of your passion

I sprang forth to witness
    you come & go from the house
        in Havana you bought
            on your policeman's salary,
            when the daily work got rough,

rougher than you'd imagine.
    Twice I listened, twice,
        when you'd scream because madness
        then, like now, was possible.
        That same scream brought us here,

to this new land. I remember too
    that in Madrid you fell on the floor
        & I ran down the apartment hallways
        in my underwear like a creature stirred
        in the night, wild-eyed.

Something went wrong.
    But your heart kick-started once more,
        after the CPR & the familial tenderness,
        for to have lost you, well . . .
        Now here we are,

more than twenty years later
well into your half-time.
It is true: one doesn't get any younger,
one doesn't learn new tricks
& the years keep gnawing.

I still watch you come & go,
& from the distance of five hundred miles
some of your advice
has become balled-up fists
that still box my ears with truths.

Prayer

my mother stands next to my father's bed
at Palm Springs General Hospital, Hialeah,

Florida, her back toward his sleep. The clip-
clop soft of her tongue as it finds the groove

of words—all that "s" in the hissing.
Which psalm? Which prayer? My father

lost to the dream of some azure land,
of fertile fields, then the phone rings.

"Fine. Here. Good," my mother says,
not really deterred from her prayer.

My father dreams of a man: active, vital,
prone to sudden bursts of passion

and nostalgia, never happy, not religious
in his youth, but now, now prayer helps

prop him up against all that ails him.
We are waiting for lab results from Jackson

Memorial, hoping the cancer in his colon
hasn't spread to any other vital organs.

Little did we know that a day later, he'd die
of a massive coronary, a blood clot.

For now, my mother's prayer seems to do
its work of lulling all of us to sleep,

to dream of some previous life
in another country, convinced that prayer,

like innocence, sees us through daily life.

Land of Plenty

ten men living in the fourth-floor
walk-up on the Bowery curse
the heat for its persistence, the flies
buzz about and land on the brim
of wax-coated cups left in the kitchen
where the men only cook noodles
in light broth, green onion, rice too,
half-naked they run into each other
in the apartment-cubicle, keeping
quiet; nobody wants to be found out
and deported, better here and this
than there and the unattainable—
at least here they can almost grasp
freedom, like the warm beer they share,
the deck of overused, sticky cards,
the black-and-white television set
upon which they watch pornography,
they take turns at the kitchen-side
urinals, or they hunt pigeons brave
enough to come near the open window.
Young, old, they share this moment,
this life, here in America, and at night
their dreams break with the gurgle
of urinals flushing, a pail of water
thrown in quickly, just like that,
like the volatility of their lives, only
roaches and rats know the trick
of their subsistence: a dream of a boat
lost on the waters, a useless map
of stars, galaxies, of no way home.

PART

Destierro

Biscayne Boulevard, Miami, 1974

Freshly arrived from Madrid, staying at my uncle's house,
    my cousin Robert and I each day ventured from the front yard
of this house on 65th and Biscayne a little further. We got away

smooth, each time closer to the strip where we saw the women
    my cousin called "hookers" and I, not speaking English yet,
asked what that meant in Spanish. He called them "*putas.*"

I understood, sort of, though I'd never seen one, but I had heard
    my parents gossip about women they knew who "received"
too many men visitors and about whom they whispered "*puta.*"

Each time, away from the watchful gaze of our parents,
    my cousin and I drew nearer to the corner motels,
next to the rows of crocus and hibiscus. At this corner,

the prostitutes hung out in shorts, lots of skin showing.
    They stood around, shifting weight from one heel
to the other. One sat on the top of a fire hydrant, legs open,

across the street, next to the newspaper dispensers. She waved
    at the cars going by, a few honked. They strut up and down
the street, careful on their high heels, dressed in tight

clothes, held by a zipper, knot or snap. Oblivious or indifferent
    to us, we were only twelve or so,
my cousin and I, and we stood by watching, shy, nervous.

These women ignored us as they tried to stop traffic, some
    did—a bearded man in a blue Spitfire, top down, cigarette
burning in his fingers—"Hey, baby," he said. "How much?

What's the cost of fun these days?" I didn't understand
    what they were saying, these men, these women, to each other
and I kept asking my cousin for translation as if we were watching

a dubbed movie, and it was like one, foreign, hard to follow,
        awkward. "The johns," my cousin said and laughed. No
translation for that, these men who came to this corner.

Each time we came nearer we were called back by my uncle's
        dog, a poodle with a bell around its neck, and its jingle
warned us that we'd gone too far, out for a walk, my uncle

headed our way, then we'd hear his whistle for it, for us,
        to come back closer to home, the knot of excitement in our
throats, the fist of nerves in our guts. "Soon," my cousin

sighed. There was the whistle again, bringing us back
        from the wild neon, the precipice we came to know
as our manhood at the corner of 65th & Biscayne.

Muñeca, Huntington Park,
Nineteen Eighty Something

It was during the Summer Olympics
in Los Angeles that my father met her;
she came over with her then boyfriend/
lover, some guy they called "Niño."

They called her Muñeca, which means
doll, and the three men at the party
swooned over her. My sister, mother
and me watched these three grown

men outside on the lawn running
around her, "the witch" as we came
to know her. They smelled something
about her, like cats do, my mother

said. She promised never to have
any other parties—that was it, no more
free food and sangrias for that bitch.
A year later, my father left my mother

for Muñeca, who had left Niño
in what rumor held to be a pretty
ugly sight: clothes on the lawn, broken
windows, dented car fender, bruises.

Ugly. My father came home from work
one afternoon, told my mother like
he was saying goodbye to strangers,
got in the car and took off. I watched

from the living room window, across
the lawn as the car picked up speed
then turned for good at the corner.
I can't remember if my mother cried,

but we lived on, knowing that the gap
existed, and my mother and sister never
mentioned his name again. At night,
in the dark of my bedroom, I looked

at the picture of my mother and father
in Havana, outside the building where
they said they got married. And I thought
of Muñeca, how she had come that one

time and changed our lives forever.
Powder-smooth cleavage and emerald
eyes, I remember how she tilted her neck
as she sipped sangria to show off her chest.

Her manicured nails gripped and clinked
the glass like a bell. And I promised
myself I would forget that Aren't-I-wonderful
look, her high cheeks, the way she hissed

words through her teeth. Of course, her affair
with my father lasted only a couple of years.
She left him like my mother said she would,
and my father could never come back.

The weakness of men, my mother called it,
for which he would pay and pay and pay.
He came by every so often to say hello,
or at school to buy me and my sister lunch.

Years later, when my sister moved out,
I went to college in Florida. My mother
stayed in California and lived alone.
My father died of a stroke.

Once in Miami at La Carreta, I was there
with my fiancée eating dinner, and I got up
to go to the bathroom and to do so you have
to enter the cantina, a smoky dark cavern.

Muñeca sat at the bar working on her vermouth.
A man kept his head buried in her breasts.
He was drunk. She looked wasted, old and haggard.
The smoke of a burning cigar coiled in her hair.

I looked long enough to make sure it was her.
At that moment I thought of my father
and his friends that one afternoon on the lawn,
of my mother looking out at them, and she

now alone in her room in California,
Spanish soap operas on the television,
watching as bad things happen to good people.
Me, I decided long ago not to get involved,

not to let these seeds take root
in the darkness of my memory.

Song for the Royal Palms of Miami

for Gustavo Pérez Firmat

Everywhere they stand, slightly bent
against nocturnal offshore breezes,

as if strained to hear the susurrus of wind:
free, free, *libre* . . . Dear Gustavo, when

we spoke of this catatonia befallen
our fathers, this inertia of mind and spirit,

we might have second-guessed their wills,
the dregs-like residue of hope left inside them; us.

Memories against the "*ventolera*"
as my old man calls the winds of change.

Here he is at Palm Springs Hospital
recovering once again from major surgery,

this time the offensive being against colon
cancer. (Little do I know he will not,

not make it out.) Listen, we too struggle
against the uncertainty, pulled by the roots,

remembrance of our lost childhoods.

I think of you on this clear
November day, when outside the hospital

window, wind tussles the fronds
of a palm tree, not any palm tree, but a royal

palm tree, like the ones all over that island.
My father knows its name: *palmera*.

So does yours. They know the *palmiche*,
fed to pigs to fatten them up, the leaves

of the fronds used to make good hats,
the earthwormlike trunks can be dug

out to make canoes.

 They are everywhere
these slender giants, proud, resolute

against the ravages of weather and time.
I say they are built to survive everything.

I say today they are mile markers of our
fathers' trip through exile, monuments

to their bravura of spirit—they've been planted
here to remind all of us of the long way home.

Symbiotic

How does a deer go into the dark?
Moving in the stillness of a foggy night

only to be crushed by the fender
of an eighteen-wheeler. What blinds it

isn't light, but a yearning to cross
the highway. The deer stands there, on edge,

momentarily gnaws at sweet dandelion.
Under the stars, it inches closer to the line

it must not cross. Then the screech of wheels.
Now, there by the side of the same road,

perched on the deer's exposed and broken
rib cage, a crested caracara:

regal, resolute, bent on scavenge.
It does thorough work. Its feathers shine hot

in the morning sun, devoid of blood.
On its already red face not a trace of guilt

or difference. This is a bird unlike any other,
a dead deer like countless others roadside.

Nothing out of place in this Texas
land of open sky, wide blue that makes the eye

water in its blueness from such a distance,
and my father, dead on a hospital bed,

his eyes dulled to the fluorescent lights.
A nurse asks if he was an organ donor,

his corneas so precious. I say no, not his eyes.
Anything but his eyes because with his eyes,

animals have learned to creep forth from the deepest
woods to find the solace of final rest on the edges

of these roads in this land so many strangers,
after difficult crossings, have learned to call home.

Gallos finos

My father longed for the wild days of cockfighting
  in Cuban heat where he was born—the whiskey smell
    of the cocks' damp feathers, their slick smoothness,
  radiant flash in the bright sun—he knew too much
about the birds, their history, like how the Chinese

bred and cross-bred the jungle fowl, *Gallus gallus*,
  with Himalayan bankivas for lightning speed and flying,
    swift kicks, and with Malay birds for strength and wallop.
  They taught them the right skills of a mean fighter,
the punch, feint, roll, and *salto*. They marched them

though gamecock exercise, trimmed their blood-red wattles
  and combs, and stuffed dried chilies up their cloacas.
    A few thousand generations later in Cuba, the result
  was obvious in how to take two birds, program them
to kill each other, each a shimmered pulse of instinct,

training, and breeding, the dust from the pits rising;
  he loved that smell, my father, of when the birds eyed
    each other and charged, that moment of determined malice
  and viciousness, of these two roosters matched by weight,
given identical weapons attached to their cut-off bony

back spurs, strapped knives or gaffs, razor-sharp, like curved
  ice picks, onto their stumps, into an explosion of lost feathers,
    a flurry of beak and leg, a controlled storm of anger,
  until the one bird remained standing, or fled, and the fight
came to an end, this pure act of endurance, like any other,

like the other Cuban men he knew who'd emigrated
  to the United States against all odds, in the pursuit
    of something better, and anyway he remembered
  as a way to keep going in this land, because he knew
he could not breed these birds in the apartment he shared

with my mother in Hialeah, but dreamt instead of those days,
  those days of cockfighting in the glitter of his youth.

Fuel

Once when I was seven
and we lived in Cuba,
my father cut his finger
    on a rusty nail
of the chicken coop;
he pressed on it
until a drop
of crimson blood
formed, then fell
to darken the dirt–
    "See that?"
He said. "That's fuel."
I didn't understand.
When he died
in Miami thirty
years later,
    of a massive
coronary, the doctor
who performed
the Code Blue—
massaged his heart—
and failed, hurried
to where my mother
    and I waited
in the chapel.
Distressed, he showed
us his cupped hands,
when his fingers,
    unfurled
like petals,
his palms revealed ashes,
these dying embers,
    my father's
message to us
from the afterlife:
fare for all of us
to cross the dark
    together.

Nostalgia

Father's musky shirt
    hung behind the bathroom door,
        his boots, caked with mud,
            sat flapped over like dog's ears

under the sink. Everywhere in house
    there was him: the smell of his sweat,
        his cigarettes, his lighter,
            the pocket chain,

his wallet made of horsehide
    sagged in the back pocket
        of his stained work khakis.
            Often, when he suffered

an asthma attack, he sat in the dark
    of the living room, listened to rain,
        or crickets, or frogs,
            classical music,

the hiss of its static as it came from the old
    Marconi radio next to the empty
        fish tank. He became a ghost
            in his own house.

I stayed awake for as long as he did, listening too.
    The mosquito netting billowed over my bed
        hung from the ceiling and the corners
            of the room, the whisper

of his voice as he spoke to my mother
    about his fears, his dreams, aspirations,
        the possibility of dead ends,
            madness and dying.

My mother, a widow now, lives alone
   in Hialeah, Florida, with his belongings:
      his clothes, shoes, cufflink collection.
         She refuses to part

with anything, as though these are the objects,
   the way he smelled in them,
      that keep her going. For me,
         I have my own stuff,

one day when I too am gone from the world,
   my daughters will hold up the many papers,
      smoldering ashes in their hands,
         pages upon pages

and perhaps feel my breath against their faces,
   against the ravages of forgetting.

Mistranslation of Fire

A Cuban man,

fresh from the island,

lives with his mother,

one day gets a job

at which he fails

and *"El Manager"*

tells the man today

is his last day,

that he is fired,

and the man,

translates the word

into Spanish,

thinks of fire:

"Eres la candela,"

a compliment;

happy, he hurries

home to tell

his mother

how good

he's done.

Cuban American Gothic

My father stands next to my mother,
both in the simple stained work clothes

they wore to their factory jobs,
instead of sitting next to the Singer

overlap sewing machine, zippers
snaking all around her, she bends

in the background; beyond her a storm
rages, lightning fractures opaque skies,

while my father, instead of cutting denim
for pattern jeans, cradles an armful

of mason jars filled with blue fractal
light, bolts of lightning captured

for all time; in the distance, the bad weather
so absolute, this rite of passage from their

immigrant lives—*la vida dura*, my father
calls it—this skeletal American landscape

exposed by lightning, this flash of longing,
as if by X-ray, in this new foreign town,

against the ravages of time and hard work.

Song to the Sugar Cane

At Publix today with my daughters
I spotted the green stalks of sugar cane,

tucked under the boxed Holland tomatoes,
ninety-eight cents a stalk. I grabbed the three

left and brought them home. My daughters,
born in the United States, unlike me, stand

in the kitchen in awe as I take the serrated
knife and peel away the hard green layer

exposing the fibrous white, pure slices.
"Here," I say, "nothing is ever as sweet as this."

We stand in the kitchen and chew slices
of sugar cane as I tell them this was my candy

when I was a kid growing up in Havana,
this was the only constant sweetness

in my childhood. This delicious, sweet stalk.
You chew on a piece to remember how

to love what you can't have all the time.

The Trouble with Frogs

It's irrational, I know, like the fear of flying
        or high places,
but irresistible nonetheless, for frogs hide
        in the luscious green
of the plantain's fronds. There, they nest
        and call out
for nuptial visitations. Become invisible against
        the corrugated tin
of the outhouse at my grandmother's house,
        then jump . . .
The neighborhood kids catch them and put them
        down my shirt
and in my pants. Who understands the terror
        of this cold and clammy
thing moving against the skin? All the time the child
        thinks there is no return
from such fear. At night beyond the mosquito net,
        they call out.
From Havana to Tallahassee,
        frogs have evolved
into this fear of a childhood not lived,
        not remembered,
but out there, in the distance, they call; they beckon
        no matter how far I travel,
I cannot escape this trouble with frogs.
        All I can do
is embrace the fact that they are there,
        like the past,
calling out, beckoning for the mind to leap.

Relic Left Over from the Aftermath of the Cuban Revolution

or why Communism didn't work,
it is plain, writes a cousin

from Cuba, brave enough
to fool the censors: we ride

these ten-seater Chinese
bikes. Picture this, ten people,

the pedaller, the other eight
watching the guy in front

build up a sweat, pedal happy,
and the last guy, now he's made

it look easy, all he does is lean
back and enjoy the Havana breeze.

We've become an island
of hungry, frenzied bicyclists

with much to invent, nothing
to look forward to, no place

to go, but look at our legs,
we are the envy of the world.

Views of a Broken Maximum Leader, or No Absolution in History

Looks down the barrel of a Soviet-made rifle,
cigar tubes tucked deep in his uniform shirt pocket,
the target a stuffed Yankee scarecrow.

Exiled in Mexico, he knelt on sand,
one of the few times pictured in a suit,
next to a Mexican boy with *sarape* & *sombrero*.

A lit cigar in the corner of his mouth, hair blown
back as though he rode a hundred miles
on horseback, thick black glass frames.

Instructs rebel recruits in the Cuban countryside,
a twig with which he scratches logistical attack
maps on the dry earth. Delighted, Che looks on.

The white doves didn't know what they were doing
when they flew up on the podium and the one
landed on his shoulder long enough to shit there.

A sign, maybe. Surrounded by school children
during his visit to Washington D.C., a couple
of kids yank on his beard to make sure it isn't fake.

At the United Nations, the Ezra Pound-like madness
already in his eyes, an I-will-rant-and-rave grin
on his bloodless lips, above him the UN seal as halo.

A Hitler-like pose at the podium, the half-moons
of sweat darken the green of his armpits. At Latin
American Stadium, he pitches to an invisible batter,

swings the bat to an invisible pitch. Strike three.
With smiling nuns, imagine? Cutting sugar cane.
With Papa Hemingway as he leans in closer

to hear Ernest whisper: "You too will lose, you too."
With Che and brother Raúl on the tarmac,
a moment of speculation during the Bay of Pigs.

Marlin fishing with Che in Barlevento, 1960.
Nothing caught, nothing brought back to cook.
Nikita Khrushchev hugs him after a kiss,

gets cigar tube to poke El Toro Ruso's eye.
The shoe banging at the UN's podium
was El Caballo's idea. Nikita *tiene cojones*.

At Plaza José Martí, a whirlwind of words
asunder, like spooked Brahman bulls, no more
eight-hour speeches about Yankee imperialism.

Charm or enigma gone, he leans back, his old,
worn body, still in uniform, a barnacle
stuck to the hull of his long-ago sunken ship.

Dementia comes to those who wait. See it
in his sharpened nails, his upward-curved eyebrows,
the dim in his eyes, the fade-to-black of lights.

No way for history to absolve you? No way.

A Song On The End Of The Cuban Revolution

After Czeslaw Milosz

On the day Castro dies or flees
the zun zun hovers
       by the hibiscus flower,
the Russian boats on the harbor,
those that remain, sink to become reefs;
delighted, the manatee and cayman return,
the *tomeguines* and rainbow bunting nest in peace,
and the lizard will cease to change colors.

On the day of the end of the Cuban Revolution,
men, women and children gather in the fields,
in the city streets, under the fallen propaganda,
torn banners and posters, the *guajiros* play
their *décimas* on their guitars. The *son* returns
to the island, the *maniceros* resume their chants.
The laughter of the maracas and the calling
of the tumba drums rises above all clatter
       and human waking.

And those here and there who expect thunder
and the storm of vendettas are disappointed.
And those who expected bloodshed
       are disappointed.
I do not believe it is occurring now.
As long as the cane and tobacco are in the fields,
as long as the Cuban parrots are nesting,
       as long as children suckle
everyone wants to believe it is happening now.

Only an ash-haired *babalao*, prophet soothsayer,
never too busy to read his cowry shells
repeats and translates what all those sounds
       he is hearing mean:

There will be no better change in the world.
There will be no better change in the world.

Acknowledgments

Grateful acknowledgment is made to the editors and publishers of the following reviews and journals where some of these poems first appeared (sometimes in slightly different form):

Apalachee Quarterly, Atom Mind, Cedar Hill Review, Chachalaca Poetry Review, Clackamas Literary Review, Confrontation, Confluence, Crazyhorse, 5 AM, Gulf Stream Magazine, Hayden's Ferry Review, Interim, Luna, New Orleans Review, Notre Dame Review, Ontario Review, Orange Willow Review, Piedmont Literary Review, Poetry Journal, Poet Lore, Prairie Schooner, Red Cedar Review, Red Palm Review, Salmagundi, San Diego Writer's Monthly, Shenandoah, The Sow's Ear Review, Tampa Review, The American Voice, The Bloomsbury Review, The Caribbean Writer, The Chariton Review, The Ohio Review, The Ledge, The New Laurel Review, Washington Square, Westview, Witness, and *Yefief.*

A small number of these poems first appeared in different form in *Garabato Poems,* a limited edition book published by Wings Press, San Antonio, 1998 and in *Spared Angola: Memories from a Cuban-American Childhood,* published by Arte Público Press, University of Houston, Houston, Texas, 1997.

I would like to thank Ryan G. Van Cleave for his astute editorial suggestions and for taking the time to help proof and organize the manuscript. It was during an intensive poetry exchange between us over a period of one semester that most of these poems were written. Other poets helped as well: Jacqueline D. Parker, Michael Dennison, and Wasabi Watanabe Kanastoga. Also, as always I would like to thank David Kirby, Barbara Hamby, Luis J. Rodríguez, Bryce Milligan, Ray González, Judith Ortiz Cofer, Naomi Shihab Nye, Juan Felipe Herrera, Leroy V. Quintana, Adrián Castro, Pablo Medina, Roberto G. Fernández, Gustavo Pérez Firmat, Ricardo Pau-Llosa, Richard Blanco, and Víctor Hernández Cruz for their ongoing support and inspiration. To them all I give a million thanks. Many thanks go to Karen Van Hooft, Karen Akins, and Gary Keller for believing in this book. Most of this collection was made possible by a Florida State Individual Artist Grant from the Division of Cultural Affairs of the State of Florida. Finally, deepest gratitude and love to my wife and daughters and family who always provide the muse, music, and understanding.